Kindergarten Symphony

Kindergarten Symphony

(An ABC Book)

David H. Rosen

FOREWORD BY
Thomas Moore

RESOURCE *Publications* • Eugene, Oregon

KINDERGARTEN SYMPHONY
(An ABC Book)

Resource Publications
An Imprint of Wipf and Stock Publishers
199 W. 8th Ave., Suite 3
Eugene, OR 97401

www.wipfandstock.com

PAPERBACK ISBN: 978-1-5326-8330-5
HARDCOVER ISBN: 978-1-5326-8331-2
EBOOK ISBN: 978-1-5326-8332-9

Manufactured in the U.S.A.

This is dedicated to all kindergarteners,
their parents and teachers.

Foreword

DAVID ROSEN'S NEW BOOK shows that he is a lover of children and animals and wants you to be one, too. This book is quite simple on the surface, an alphabet of animals with a one-word epithet for each. But I sense something lurking behind the simple facade.

Consider Zen Zebra. You might think that this book is a simple children's book, just as the Zen master insists that Zen is nothing more than sitting. It's a mere alphabet of animals, but when I finished reading it I felt hypnotized. I had gone through a long list of animals and looked into their faces, nothing to order them other than the first letter of their species name. So simple. But I've already written many more words than David Rosen did, so there is an element of irony there, too. The foreword is much longer and infinitely more complicated than the book.

The adjective describing each animal comes from the imagination, not science. So what we have here is an imaginary zoo, a catalogue of animals that are not as literal as those studied in a university. In the Middle Ages clever writers depicted animals in this way—half real and half imaginary.

Here you can picture an animal and imagine it having human personality quirks. But what is going on when we anthropomorphize animals, give them a human psychology and abilities? Maybe we're affirming the close tie we have with them and the idea that they are as sensitive and inventive as we are.

Rosen didn't have to say all this, but his inspiration to give us an alphabet of animals to contemplate, with obvious fun and hidden seriousness, gives his book dimension and layers. Read it a few times and notice what happens to you. It will put you under a spell.

My favorite animal is Xenial Xerus. I didn't know either word, but then I realized that xenial must be related to xenophobia, its opposite. Now I love the word "xenial" and hope to use it in conversations with other humans. I have a whole new alphabet to enrich my life and, remembering the xerus, help me maintain a xenial outlook.

Thomas Moore

Author of *The Care of the Soul*

Acknowledgments

I'D LIKE TO THANK Bonnie Sheehey and Rebekah Sinclair for their assistance with this fun project. I'm very thankful to Wipf & Stock publishers for their careful attention to detail and help with this book. In particular, I thank James Stock and Jim Tedrick. Finally, I appreciate Thomas Moore for writing such a creative foreword to this book.

A Book is Born

THIS BOOK GREW OUT of deprivation. You see, I never went to kindergarten, so it was always something I wanted. But, it was inaccessible. In 1949, when I was finally old enough to go, we lived in Big Spring, Texas, and they had never heard of such a thing. The alternative was a crude daycare center with an alcoholic caretaker who passed out on a dilapidated couch while we ran around like wild puppies. Back in rural New York, where I was from, they did have a garden of children. When I was in preschool, we were all looking forward to finally going to a real school and just as it was within my tiny reach, we moved. I wondered why we didn't stay in New York. I didn't understand why my father wanted to move our family so far from that idyllic place on the Boston Post Road. One memory of New York that has stuck with me is about my mother's dear friend, Virginia, who would communicate with ants. She would say quietly to them, "Please go out the way you came in." Then I watched in amazement: it was a miracle. The ants turned right around and exited just the way they came in.

I remember loving ABC books as a way to master the alphabet. But do we need another? Yes, as each one, like every person, is different. In this book, my goal is to establish a harmony of images and sounds through the alphabet. In that way, Kindergarten Symphony was conceived and nurtured through its long gestation period.

A is for Advancing Ant

B is for Belching Bull

C is for Chewing Cow

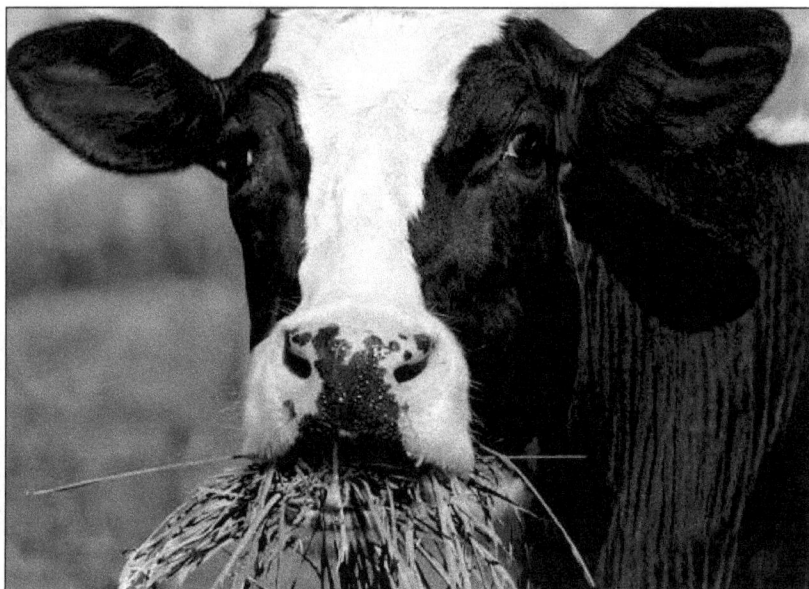

D is for Dancing Dog

E is for Eccentric Elephant

F is for Fascinating Fox

G is for Giddy Giraffe

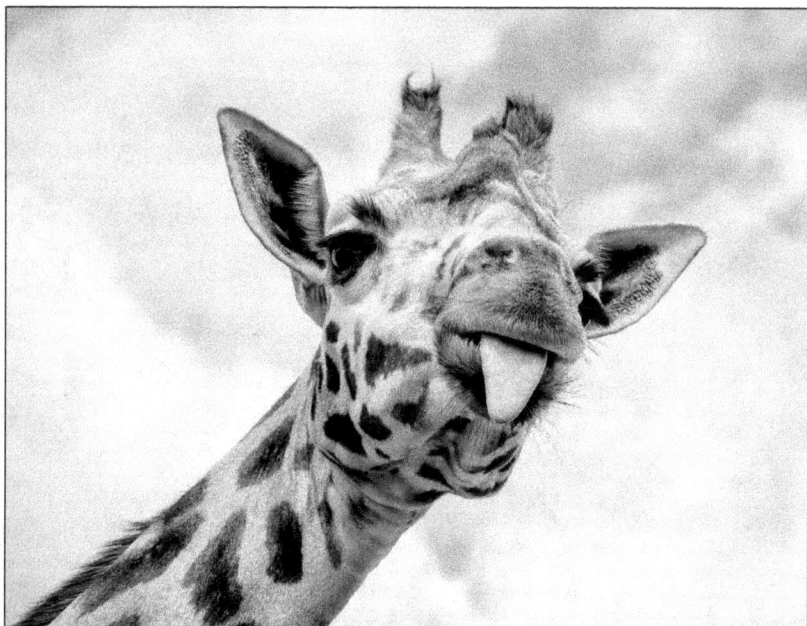

H is for **Happy Hippo**

I is for Interesting Iguana

J is for Joyful Jaguar

K is for Kangaroo King

L is for Lazy Lizard

M is for Magical Moose

N is for Napping Newt

O is for **Observing Owl**

P is for **Prickly Porcupine**

Q is for Quail Queen

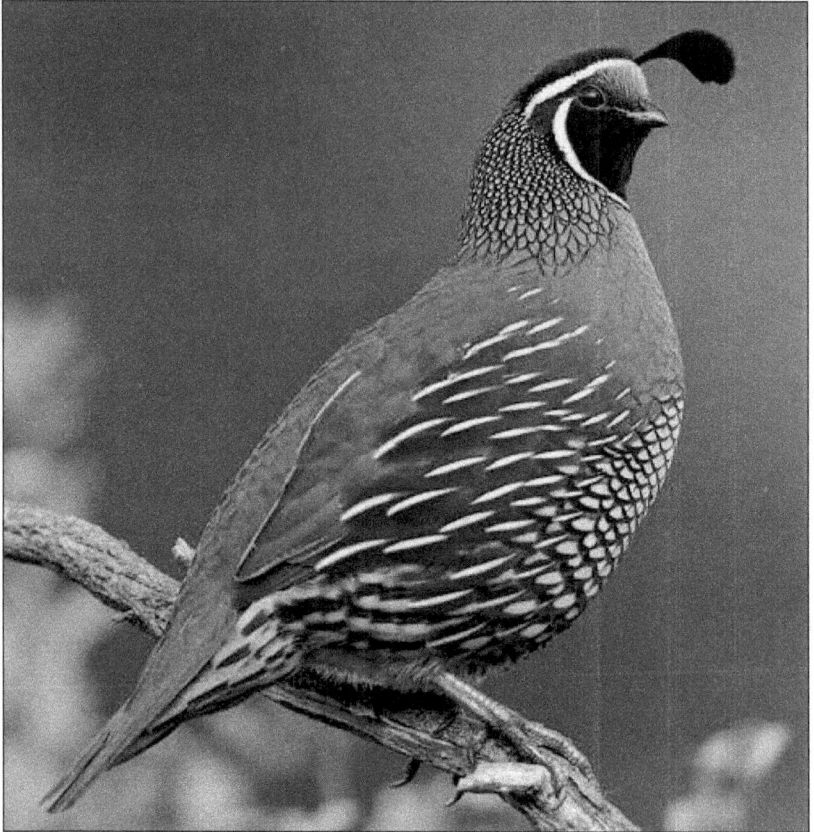

R is for **Racing Rabbit**

S is for Slithering Snake

T is for Terrific Tiger

U is for Unique Unicorn

V is for Visiting Vulture

W is for Wonderful Weasel

X is for Xenial Xerus

Y is for Yelling Yak

Z is for Zen Zebra